THIS LAND CALLED AMERICA: **MINNESOTA**

CREATIVE EDUCATION

Published by Creative Education
P.O. Box 227, Mankato, Minnesota 56002
Creative Education is an imprint of The Creative Company
www.thecreativecompany.us

Book and cover design by Blue Design (www.bluedes.com)
Art direction by Rita Marshall
Printed in the United States of America

Photographs by Alamy (Scott Kemper), Corbis (Layne Kennedy,
Richard Hamilton Smith), Getty Images (Waring Abbott/Michael
Ochs Archives; Bill Alkofer; Tom Bean; KAREN BLEIER/AFP; George
Catlin, Melanie Stetson Freeman/The Christian Science Monitor, Jeff
Gross, James Hager, Hulton Archive, Imagno, Curtis Johnson, Mitch
Kezar, CRAIG LASSIG/AFP, Fred Mayer, MPI; Michael Quinton, Ryan/
Beyer, George Skadding/Time & Life Pictures, Time Life Pictures/Time
Magazine, Copyright Time Inc./Time Life Pictures)

Library of Congress Cataloging-in-Publication Data
Peterson, Sheryl.
Minnesota / by Sheryl Peterson.
p. cm. — (This land called America)
Includes bibliographical references and index.
ISBN 978-1-58341-648-8
1. Minnesota—Juvenile literature. I. Title. II. Series.
F606.3.P48 2008
977.6—dc22   2007019625

First Edition
9 8 7 6 5 4 3 2 1

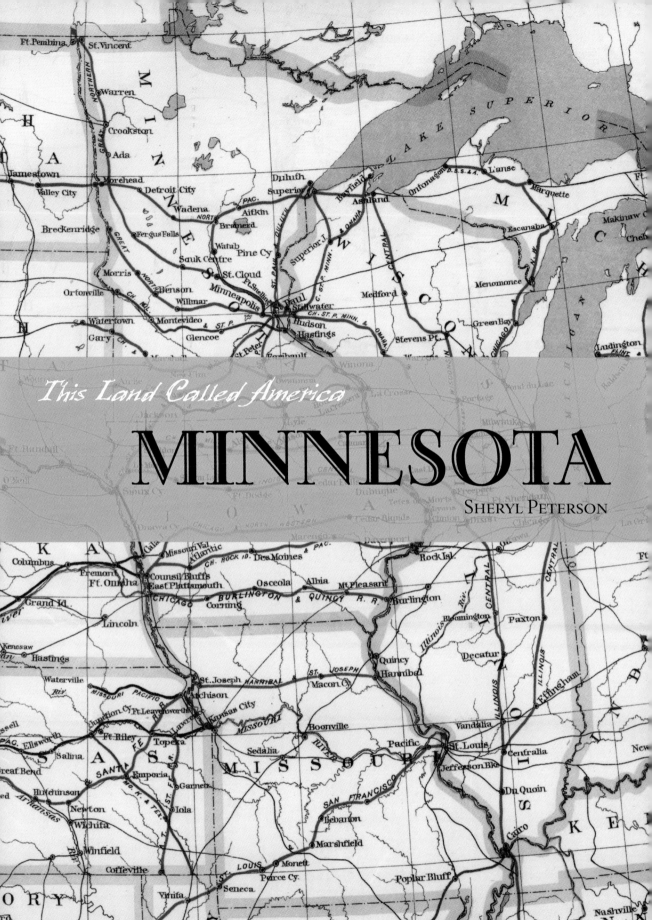

This Land Called America

MINNESOTA

SHERYL PETERSON

This Land Called America

Minnesota

SHERYL PETERSON

It's fishing season in Minnesota. A bucket of minnows bounces in the bottom of a small aluminum boat. Cool breezes ruffle the lake surface. A bald eagle soars over tall Norway pines as a fisherman feels a tug on his line. His fishing buddy grabs the net and scoops up a flopping walleye. It's a keeper! Tonight at the family cabin, fresh fish will be served in the screened-in porch. Later, when the pesky mosquitoes have gone to bed, everyone will roast marshmallows by the campfire. While loons call hauntingly across the water, family members will share their exciting Minnesota fish stories.

YEAR
1680   Father Louis Hennepin discovers St. Anthony Falls where present-day Minneapolis is located.
EVENT

- 5 -

From Pines to Prairies

Hundreds of years ago, only Dakota (or Sioux) Indians lived in Minnesota. Tribe members hunted buffalo and fished. They picked blueberries and harvested northern beds of wild rice. Minnesota natives lived in warm animal-skin teepees that they could pack up and move easily.

In 1679, French explorer Daniel Greysolon, Sieur du Luth, crossed Minnesota in search of a route to the Pacific Ocean. He did not find the route, but he claimed the region for France anyway. In 1680, a priest named Louis Hennepin traveled up the Mississippi River from Iowa. He discovered a 65-foot (20 m) drop in the river and named it St. Anthony Falls. The Falls are now surrounded by the present-day city of Minneapolis.

During the 1700s and 1800s, French-Canadian traders called voyageurs paddled their birch-bark canoes into Minnesota. They traveled along the north shore of Lake Superior and the border with Canada. The voyageurs traded with the Indians for beaver furs.

Although Minnesota's natives no longer live in teepees (above), they continue to harvest wild rice (opposite) as they have for centuries.

YEAR
1803   The United States purchases the Louisiana Territory, which includes Minnesota.
EVENT

YEAR

1820   Fort Snelling is built to help the U.S. take control of the area's fur trade.

EVENT

State bird: common loon

The Ojibwe (or Chippewa) people moved into Minnesota from the East Coast. They traded furs in exchange for French metal tools, weapons, and beads. By 1800, the Ojibwe occupied most of the forests of the north. But in 1803, President Thomas Jefferson made a land deal with France called the Louisiana Purchase. It made Minnesota part of the U.S., and Indian tribes were soon forced to give up most of their lands.

In 1820, the U.S. Army built a frontier outpost called Fort Snelling at a point where the Mississippi and Minnesota rivers met. The fort helped protect pioneers as they traveled west. In the 1830s, large groups of immigrants from Norway, Sweden, and Germany moved into Minnesota.

In 1840, the city of St. Paul was founded on the banks of the Mississippi River. Soon, Minneapolis was created on the opposite side of the river. The towns became known as the "Twin Cities." In 1858, Minnesota became America's 32nd state. Henry Sibley, a former fur trader, served as the state's first governor. By 1860, more than 172,000 people had settled in Minnesota.

The American Civil War started in 1861. Southern states wanted to keep their decades-old practice of slavery, but Northern states wanted to end slavery. Minnesota was the first state to send troops to fight for the North. After the

Fort Snelling (opposite) was originally named Fort St. Anthony, but its name was changed in 1825.

North won in 1865, more settlers moved to Minnesota. Some people grew wheat, while others ground wheat into flour in the big Minneapolis mills.

By 1862, the Dakota Indians had been forced onto a small reservation in southern Minnesota. When their crops failed, a fierce battle called the Dakota Conflict broke out. The Dakota people fought U.S. soldiers for six weeks. Hundreds of people were killed on both sides, and the Dakota lost the rest of their land.

Pioneer life on the prairie was hard. People lived in houses made of sod (pieces of earth) or crude log cabins. Huge clouds of grasshoppers often destroyed their crops. A disease called scarlet fever took many lives. Winters were long and bitterly cold.

In 1893, Minnesota businessman James J. Hill, called the "Empire Builder," completed the Great Northern Railway. It ran all the way from St. Paul to Seattle, Washington, on the West Coast. The long railroad made it easy to travel across the American West.

YEAR

1832 Geographer Henry Schoolcraft and his native guide find the source of the Mississippi River in northern Minnesota.

EVENT

Land of Sky-Blue Waters

MINNESOTA IS BORDERED ON THE NORTH BY THE PROVINCE OF ONTARIO, CANADA. THE STATES OF NORTH AND SOUTH DAKOTA LIE TO THE WEST. IOWA IS TO THE SOUTH, AND LAKE SUPERIOR AND WISCONSIN FORM THE STATE'S EASTERN BOUNDARY.

THE LAND IS HILLY AND ROCKY IN THE NORTHEASTERN REGION OF THE STATE, WHICH CONTAINS EAGLE MOUNTAIN, THE STATE'S HIGHEST POINT (AT 2,301 FEET, OR 701 M). VAST PINE FORESTS

and sparkling lakes cover Minnesota's northern third, while the central and southwestern areas of the state have rolling plains with rich soil that is perfect for farming. Southeastern Minnesota features high bluffs and deep valleys near the Mississippi and St. Croix rivers.

Along with statues of Paul Bunyan and Babe in Bemidji, visitors can also see Paul's grave in Kelliher.

Minnesota's license plates boast that it is the "Land of 10,000 Lakes," but there may be almost twice that many. Minnesota's name comes from the Dakota word for "sky-tinted waters," and people can see the sky reflected in lakes throughout the state. Lake Superior, part of the Great Lakes chain, is the largest freshwater lake in the world. It borders such northeastern cities as Duluth.

The folktale of lumberjack Paul Bunyan and Babe the Blue Ox says that Babe's big footprints made the Minnesota lakes. The larger-than-life characters are used to explain many features of Minnesota's landscape. Visitors can see huge statues of Paul Bunyan and Babe in Bemidji and Brainerd.

The more than 10,000 lakes in Minnesota are popular destinations for fishing and recreation.

The mighty Mississippi River starts as a small stream in Itasca State Park near Bemidji. Visitors can hop across it there. Then the river flows southward for 2,552 miles (4,107 km) to New Orleans, Louisiana. The Minnesota, Red, and St. Croix are other scenic Minnesota rivers.

YEAR

1861   Minnesota becomes the first state to send troops to fight for the North in the Civil War.

EVENT

- *13* -

I n the late 1800s, parts of northern Minnesota were stripped bare of trees to make room for open-pit iron ore mining. As the iron deposits ran out, other methods of mining replaced the open pits. In the 1930s, a U.S. government program called the Civilian Conservation Corps planted more than 25 million trees in Minnesota. Almost one-third of Minnesota land is now dense forest. Hickory and oak are common in the south. The forests of the north and east have spruce, birch, and pine trees.

While central and southern Minnesota feature endless fields of corn and soybeans (opposite), the state's northern woods are dense with birch and pine trees (above).

YEAR
1894   The worst fire in Minnesota history destroys the towns of Hinkley, Sandstone, and Mission Creek.
EVENT

Minnesota forests and lakes provide homes for many wild animals. Minnesota has more timber wolves than any other state except Alaska. Canada geese, ducks, and black bears are also plentiful. In the northern regions of Minnesota, loons call across the lakes. Walleye, northern pike, and trout swim below. Eagles glide above the St. Croix and Mississippi rivers in search of fish. In the fall, many Minnesotans hunt for ring-necked pheasants, ruffed grouse, and white-tailed deer in the harvested fields and woods.

The common loon can dive as deep as 250 feet (76 m) to search for food underwater.

Tall prairie grasses once covered the southern and western parts of the state. Today, wild irises, cattails, and wood lilies grow around farmland. Agriculture remains the backbone of Minnesota's economy. Farmers grow corn, soybeans, and wheat. They raise hogs, cows, and turkeys. In western Minnesota's Red River Valley, potatoes, sunflowers, and sugar beets are grown.

Animals and crops manage to stay alive in a state infamous for its cold weather. Minnesota receives an average of 20 inches (51 cm) of snow per year in the southern parts and up to 70 inches (178 cm) in the north. The northernmost city of International Falls is called the "Icebox of the Nation."

YEAR
1898 Stone carvings found near Alexandria suggest that the Vikings may have explored Minnesota in 1362.
EVENT

Hardy Minnesotans

MOST OF MINNESOTA'S EARLY SETTLERS CAME FROM NORWAY, SWEDEN, GERMANY, AND IRELAND. IN THE LATE 1900S, PEOPLE ARRIVED FROM MEXICO, SOUTHEAST ASIA, AND RUSSIA. RECENTLY, MANY HMONG (*MUNG*) IMMIGRANTS HAVE MOVED FROM LAOS TO MINNESOTA IN SEARCH OF A BETTER LIFE. TODAY, THE TWIN CITIES AREA

has more Hmong residents than any other U.S. city. Only two percent of Minnesotans are African American. Many Minnesotans live in cities or small towns. Only one-third of the population lives in the country.

Immigrant students who do not know English are placed in special English Language Learner classes.

Wherever they live, Minnesotans are proud of their schools. The state has a strong public school system. The University of Minnesota opened in 1851. It is one of the largest universities in the country and an important research center. Minnesota has more than 100 other colleges and universities as well.

Once lakes in Minnesota are frozen enough, people can drill holes for ice fishing.

Minnesotans love the outdoors. They don't let chilly winters keep them inside. Instead, they snowmobile and ice

If people do not own a cabin, they can easily rent one at one of the state's more than 1,100 resorts.

fish in the winter. Scandinavian immigrants brought cross-country skiing to Minnesota. Today, there are more than 2,500 miles (4,023 km) of ski trails in the state. Lutsen, near Grand Marais on Lake Superior's north shore, is a popular downhill skiing and snowboarding resort.

During the summers, many Minnesotans head "up north" to their lake cabins to go boating. In 1922, a young man named Ralph Samuelson strapped on a pair of skis. As he skied behind a boat across Minnesota's Lake Pepin, the sport of water-skiing was born that day.

Most Minnesotans either live in the Twin Cities or travel there often. The cities are a cultural center of the Upper Midwest. Besides shopping at the cities' many indoor malls, people can take in cultural attractions such as a Minnesota Orchestra concert. They can visit the American Swedish Institute or the St. Paul Science Museum. Or they can see a play at Minneapolis's famous Guthrie Theater, which produces more than 20 shows each year.

YEAR

1948   For the first time, Minnesota factories produce more goods than the state's farms.

EVENT

Folk-rock singer Bob Dylan, of Hibbing, releases his first album.

THE WORLD ACCORDING TO PEANUTS

People in Minnesota do many different jobs. Some make computers and machines. Some farm the land. Many residents work in the banking business or sell goods to people. Loggers cut and haul timber. Others make paper from pulpwood in the state's huge paper mills.

Minnesotans are creative thinkers. Each summer, the Minnesota Inventors Congress is held in the small town of Redwood Falls. People demonstrate their imaginative gadgets to curious onlookers. The inventors hope to win prizes and someday sell their creations.

Many Minnesotans have become artists or entertainers. Charles Schulz, who created Snoopy and Charlie Brown of the popular *Peanuts* cartoons, was born in Minneapolis. Singer Bob Dylan, who wrote songs such as "Like a Rolling Stone," grew up in Hibbing. And actress Judy Garland, who played Dorothy in *The Wizard of Oz*, came from Grand Rapids. Every year, Grand Rapids hosts a Judy Garland Festival, complete with visiting munchkins.

Artist Charles Schulz
created the PEANUTS
comic strip, originally
entitled LIL' FOLKS, in
1950.

YEAR

1987 The Minnesota Twins baseball team wins its first World Series.

EVENT

One of the most famous Minnesotans was Charles Lindbergh. Lindbergh grew up in Little Falls. On May 20, 1927, he made the first successful nonstop solo flight across the Atlantic Ocean. Lindbergh started in New York and, 33 hours later, landed in Paris, France. He flew his plane, the *Spirit of St. Louis*, without a parachute or night-flying equipment. "Lucky Lindy," as he was called, became a hero around the world after his historic trip.

From the far-northern birthplace of Judy Garland (above) to centrally located Little Falls, home of Charles Lindbergh (opposite), Minnesota has produced many famous people.

In 24 hours, the "Halloween Blizzard" drops two feet (60 cm) of snow over most of the state.

Stars of the North

MINNESOTANS HAVE BEAUTIFUL LAKES AND FORESTS, BUT THERE IS MUCH MORE TO SEE IN THE STATE. PEOPLE FROM ALL OVER THE WORLD VISIT THE MALL OF AMERICA, LOCATED IN BLOOMINGTON. EACH YEAR, MORE THAN 42 MILLION PEOPLE COME TO SHOP IN THE MEGA-MALL'S 520 STORES. CHILDREN AND ADULTS RIDE THE SPIRALING ROLLER COASTER AND GIANT FERRIS WHEEL OR BUILD LEGO CASTLES AT THE LEGO CENTER.

Another place that draws people to Minnesota is the Mayo Clinic in the southeastern city of Rochester. The clinic was founded by William Mayo and his two sons in 1883. It is now the largest nonprofit clinic in the world. The center does scientific research to cure diseases. People come to the Mayo Clinic from many other countries because of its reputation for solving difficult medical problems.

The Minnesota Wild team has been playing hockey at St. Paul's Xcel Energy Center since the year 2000.

Minnesotans love their professional sports teams. They put on Viking warrior horns and purple and gold clothing to cheer for football's Minnesota Vikings. They are loyal to basketball's Timberwolves and hockey's Wild, especially since Eveleth, Minnesota, is the home of the U.S. Hockey Hall of Fame. But when spring arrives, baseball fans take center stage as they cheer on their Minnesota Twins. Even though he was not born in the state, Twins center fielder Kirby Puckett was a Minnesota fan favorite. Puckett starred for the team from 1984 to 1995 and was elected to the Baseball Hall of Fame in 2001.

The Mall of America's indoor amusement park was renamed and redesigned in 2008 as Nickelodeon Universe.

Visiting the Duluth harbor is a treat for any visitor. It is exciting to watch the giant ships come and go across Lake Superior. The Aerial Lift Bridge is raised to allow ships from many nations into the harbor. The 230-foot (70 m) bridge is the tallest of its kind in the world.

North of Duluth, high on a cliff, sits Split Rock Lighthouse. It was built to help guide ships away from dangerous waters. Underground metal deposits threw off ships' compasses and caused many shipwrecks before the lighthouse was built. In 1970, the historic area was made into a park.

Voyageurs National Park, which was established in 1975, is located on the border with Canada. This national treasure preserves thousands of acres of forests and waterways that were once traveled by fur trappers. The Boundary Waters Canoe Area Wilderness (BWCAW) is near Ely in the northeastern corner of the state. There, people paddle and portage their canoes from one crystal-clear lake to another.

In the southwest corner of the state, people can visit the Jeffers Petroglyphs. There are more than 2,000 figures that are carved into the red, quartzite rocks amid the prairie grasses. Scientists believe that the drawings of buffaloes, arrows, and people may be about 5,000 years old!

At Split Rock Lighthouse State Park, visitors can tour the restored 1910 lighthouse.

YEAR
1999 The U.S. Supreme Court grants Ojibwe people the right to fish, hunt, and harvest using traditional methods.
EVENT

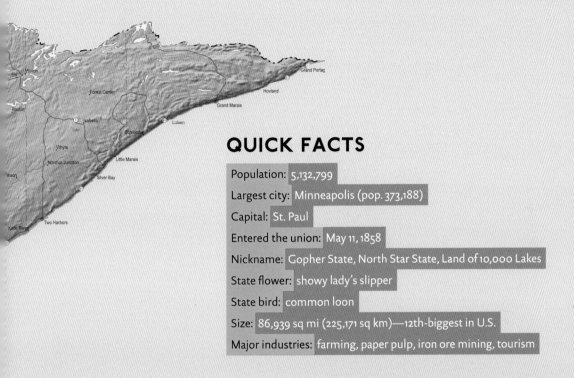

QUICK FACTS

Population: 5,132,799

Largest city: Minneapolis (pop. 373,188)

Capital: St. Paul

Entered the union: May 11, 1858

Nickname: Gopher State, North Star State, Land of 10,000 Lakes

State flower: showy lady's slipper

State bird: common loon

Size: 86,939 sq mi (225,171 sq km)—12th-biggest in U.S.

Major industries: farming, paper pulp, iron ore mining, tourism

Farther south and west is the town of Pipestone. In early days, American Indians traveled great distances to the Pipestone quarries. They gathered the special red rock, called pipestone, to make peace pipes.

Minnesota's natural beauty is one of its greatest assets. People enjoy the recreation that comes with having four unique seasons. Families fish, hike, and cheer for their favorite sports teams. The land of sky-blue waters offers endless opportunities for not only entertainment and relaxation but education and meaningful work as well. Minnesotans couldn't ask for anything more.

2004 The state's first light-rail transit system connects downtown Minneapolis to the Mall of America.

BIBLIOGRAPHY

Bruun, Erik, and Rick Peterson. *State Shapes: Minnesota*. New York: Black Dog & Leventhal Publishers, 2001.

Butler, Dori Hillestad. *M Is for Minnesota*. Minneapolis: University of Minnesota Press, 1998.

Capstone Press Geography Department. *Minnesota*. Mankato, Minn.: Bridgestone Books, 1997.

Explore Minnesota Tourism. "About Minnesota." Explore Minnesota. http://www.exploreminnesota.com.

Flynn, Dan. "Book Excerpts." *Famous Minnesotans*. http://www.thefamousminnesotans.com/index.html.

Purslow, Neil. *Minnesota*. New York: Weigl Publishing, 2000.

INDEX